For my Mother, Peggy Connolly (1929- 2011)
and my Father-in-law, Robin Denniston (1926-2012)

Paperback edition published in the UK in 2021
by Clearview Books
99 Priory Park Road, London NW6 7UX

Hardback edition published in the UK in 2012
by Clearview Books
First reprint published in the UK in 2014
Second reprint published in the UK in 2016

Cover and book design Lawrence Morton
Art Direction Lawrence Morton
Edited by Catharine Snow

A CIP record for this book is available from the British
Library.

ISBN 978-1908337 597

Printed in China

10 {

spring | spri ng | noun
a. The season after winter and before summer, in which the weather becomes warmer and vegetation begins to appear,
b. A time of growth and renewal.

46 {

summer [1] | ˈsəmər | noun
a. The usually warmest season of the year, occurring between spring and autumn or, as calculated astronomically, extending from the summer solstice to the autumnal equinox.
b. A period of fruition, fulfillment, happiness, or beauty.

84 {

autumn | ˈôtəm | noun
a. The third season of the year, when crops and fruits are gathered and leaves fall, lasting from the autumnal equinox to the winter soltice.
b. A period of maturity verging on decline.

122 {

winter | ˈwintər | noun
a. The usually coldest season of the year, occurring between autumn and spring, extending in the Northern Hemisphere from the winter solstice to the vernal equinox.
b. A period of time characterized by coldness, barrenness and conclusions.

My mother loved flowers and she made them a very normal part of everyday life. We always had flowers and plants of some sort in the house.

Most often it was just a few stems picked from the garden, or a bunch of daffodils bought from the green-grocer but, as I grew up, *the idea of bringing nature inside and observing the changing cycle of the seasons*, was a routine firmly planted in my mind.

I realise now how lucky I was.

At that stage, I never dreamt that flowers would be my career. But now it's very obvious that my whole approach has its roots in those early experiences: I still like to bring nature inside and choose seasonal, locally grown flowers whenever I can and whatever the scale of the event I've been asked to design. I still generally prefer it if the finished decorations have a simplicity and artlessness that emphasises the characteristics of the individual flowers or plants rather than any floral technical wizardry. And finally, I like it when flowers look 'comfortable' in their surroundings...when they seem the right choice for the container and for the room they are in.

I think all this is particularly important at home. In fact I like to think that home flowers are like good home cooking: Get the best, freshest, seasonal ingredients and do the least amount with them to give the best results.

Let the ingredients speak for themselves.

It's a shame when people say they get tense and nervous about arranging flowers at home.

I could completely understand it if they were being asked to decorate a vast cathedral or palace....I'd be nervous myself...but flowers at home should be a pleasure. *If you are not smiling, then you must be doing something wrong.*

To be interested in the changing seasons is a happier state of mind than to be hopelessly in love with Spring

George Santayana

There should be no real rules. There are good practices which help flowers last longer but generally speaking, I think flowers should be allowed to arrange themselves. Not making them do anything that looks artificial or unnatural sometimes requires a lot of restraint and self control!

Having the right container helps and I talk about that in more detail on page 156. It's a bit like finding beautiful plates or serving bowls to enhance food and it transforms the experience of arranging flowers.

Watching nature and being aware of the seasons also makes flower choice so much simpler.

After many years in the business, *I am still amazed how a few stems of flowers can bring life to even the most unprepossessing space*. A breath of fresh air in every sense of the word. And often it IS just a few stems that are needed.

Just a single flower can remind me of a whole garden or a few papery leaves, an autumn wood.

Many poorer cultures around the world appreciate this more than perhaps we do. Enjoying flowers is most definitely not the reserve of the rich and I hope this book will help inspire you to make them part of your everyday life too.

Winter is an etching, spring a watercolor, summer an oil painting and autumn a mosaic of them all.

Stanley Horowitz

S
P
R
I
N
G

What is it about spring?

When I first visited the London Flower Market it was spring and I was instantly hooked. I still feel the same thrill each year when I see the first boughs of blossom, a sure sign that winter is over. Or young camellia plants full of buds which slowly, sometimes infuriatingly slowly, unfurl indoors. Of course, neither of these can begin to compete for scent with jasmine plants in full flower or the first lily of the valley, possibly my favourite of all as it holds so many memories for me.

Then suddenly, there's an abundance of tulips in every colour, intensely perfumed narcissae, fritillaries and hyacinths . There are spring bulbs of every type and then, for a few short weeks, trays of auricula plants. I can't resist auricula plants and perhaps they are my favourites.

Spring, as it gathers pace, releases wave after wave of sensory delights and combines them with an innocent natural prettiness. I always try to capture that pure, unsophisticated charm when I use spring flowers and plants at home. But, above all, I relish the sense of excitement and anticipation that spring's growing bulbs and opening blossoms give me at the start of each year.

If you've never been thrilled to the very edges of your soul by a flower in spring bloom, maybe your soul has never been in bloom.

Audra Foveo

A small country church is decorated with an avenue of young crab-apple trees in old terracotta pots, underplanted with a meadow of forget-me-nots, cowslips, wild strawberries and wild grasses.

THESE
wedding flowers
appeal to me
because they are
UNPRETENTIOUS,
easy and thoughtful
in every sense of
the word

Incorporating living plants into the decorations for special occasions like this adds a completely new dimension: you can replant the crab-apple trees afterwards as life-long reminders of the day, and dismantle the plants beneath and give them to guests as well. It also follows my own philosophy of using plants organically – where they are used again after the main event.

For now the trees have been placed in these beautiful old terracotta pots. The 'meadow' beneath them is then made by grouping small cowslip, forget-me-not and wild strawberry plants with rough clumps of grasses and weeds dug up from the wilder edges of the garden to hold it all together. It's a very simple and inexpensive idea that delivers a magnificent overall effect.

Crabapple trees (malus Everest) wild strawberries (Fragaria vesca) cowslips (Primula veris) forget me nots (Myosotis sylvatica.)

IT'S RARE TO ACHIEVE THE EFFECT OF 'COLOURFULNESS' WITH FLOWERS ALONE, AND MULTI-COLOURED SCHEMES ARE PARTICULARLY TRICKY. HERE I'VE TAKEN A HANDFUL OF BURGUNDY AND ORANGE TULIPS AND PLACED THEM LIKE BOTANICAL SPECIMENS IN OLD CHEMIST'S JARS FILLED WITH TINTED WATER - A SIMPLE WAY TO ADD SEVERAL MORE SHADES TO THE PALETTE.

By contrast, the cool green fern fronds complement the intense colour of the stained glass window.

I've always been drawn to unusual colours... the kind that don't fall into any known category. So, for me, the combination of this old lustre vase and these extraordinary tulips is very special. The vase has an unusual array of tints and tones, and finding flowers to enhance them is a challenge, but the muted coppery pink of these tulips works very well. Just a handful of stems, purposely cut short so they 'clump' together, is all it takes to create a subtly magical effect.

below Tulipa 'Burnished bronze'

below This small vase of flowers is another example of the right container making a few simple flowers look better than the sum of its parts. Just a few stems of icy pink hyacinths and lime green stinking hellebore combine with the colours of the glass vase to produce something that looks harmonious and special.

below right Growing wood anemones clustered in old china compotes make great recyclable table decorations. They grow wild in many woods in their white form, but the plants are often available, both in white and blue, in florists and garden nurseries in early spring. They're shy flowers and only open in daylight so use them for lunch rather than dinner.

opposite This camellia plant is a beauty and, since camellia flowers are quite easily damaged by frost, having a small plant to bring indoors in bud is a great way to enjoy them without blemish. The oriental bronze pot is a subtle hint at the camellia's Chinese origins and contrasts well with the contemporary painting in the background.

above Hyacinths (Hyacinthus) and stinking hellebore (Helleborus feotidus) *above right* Wood anemones (Anemone blanda) *opposite* Camellia (Camellia Japonica)

The plainness of these saxifrage plants attract me as I like their abundant, cool green flowers. Here I planted them in a very contemporary white glass planter, which beautifully frames their fluffiness with clean lines and completely changes their character from soft and rustic to chic and urban. This would make a great house-warming present – a container to use for a lifetime, and plants to go into the garden later. Like many outdoor plants, they can live inside for a week or two given good light and some water.

Saxifrages (Saxifrage 'Green Ice')

Unusual plants in a striking container always make the
PERFECT GIFT

I love to use flowers thoughtfully and with meaning when designing wedding flowers and this pretty spring headdress for a young bridesmaid carries lots of symbolism from the language of flowers. Lily of the valley signifies the return of happiness, forget-me-nots for true love, ivy trails for a happy marriage and auriculas to represent the arts. The colour combination was inspired by a delicate 1930's painting of angels, found in a child's hymnbook. However the wiring for these miniature masterpieces is certainly not something you should try doing yourself. Call in the experts!

Forget-me-nots (Myosotis sylvatica) Lily of the valley (Convallaria majalis)
Auriculas (Primula auricula) and Ivy (hedera Hibernica)

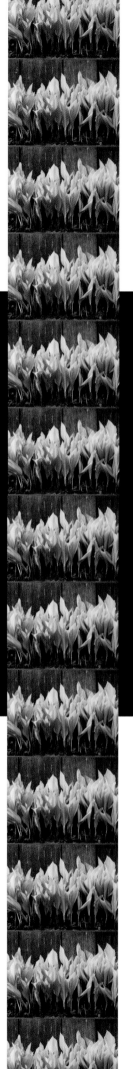

The meaning of flowers is even more important for the bride's bouquet, and this one is a scented treat. Made with two of my favourite spring flowers, jasmine and lily of the valley, the former denotes 'amiability' while the latter symbolises 'the return of happiness' or 'you have made my life complete'.

The flowers have been simply tied into a fluid, flowing bundle (very easy to do with the shapely trails of jasmine) and held together with ivory silk ribbons. I love to cut lily of the valley from growing plants which can then be planted out. They'll flower, with a bit of luck, on every anniversary.

Lily of the valley (Convallaria majalis) and Jasmine (Jasminium polyanthum)

Flowering plum (Prunus pissardii nigra)

NOTHING EPITOMIZES SPRING MORE THAN BLOSSOM. I LOVE EACH AND EVERY VARIETY AS IT COMES INTO ITS OWN, BUT PERHAPS NOTHING IS QUITE SO UPLIFTING AS WATCHING THE FIRST PIECE OF SINGLE BLOSSOM SLOWLY OPENING AT HOME. THEN YOU FEEL THAT SPRING IS REALLY ON THE WAY EVEN IF SNOW IS FALLING OUTSIDE.

Clematis plants (Clematis cartmanii Pixie)

In this age of INSTANT BEAUTY, many garden plants are sold in full flower. I love to buy them like that and *have them inside* for a week or so before planting them *permanently outside.*

For instance, I bought these PRETTY & CLEMATIS plants found a perfect *temporary home* for them in this square LOG BASKET.

We're all guilty of trying too hard sometimes, and avoid the simple and obvious in an effort to impress. This soft green helexine or 'mind-your-own-business' is one of my favourite plants for indoors. Its easy, round shape is very sculptural to look at yet it never looks contrived.

Given regular water and good non-direct light, it can be a very long lasting houseguest and I always have a few plants to dot around.

A single large plant like this one is perfect in a hall or on a side table, whilst a row of smaller helexines makes a great linear arrangement for a long dining table.

Mind your own business (Helxine Soleirolia)

This arrangement is a subtle blend of silvery
grey whitebeam with some dark and mysterious
Persian fritillaries and a few stems of fresh green
Solomon's seal. Each ingredient, artlessly
arranged in old glass pickle jars full of water,
complements the other perfectly.

Whitebeam is a wonderful tree in spring, both
growing and as a long lasting cut branch for
indoors. Its young leaves are a soft green-grey
with downy white undersides and it goes well
with, and flatters, almost every spring colour
you care to think of.

Whitebeam (Sorbus aria 'Lutescens'),
Persian fritillaries (fritallaria Persica) and
Solomon's seal (Polygonatum odoratum)

PURPLE LILAC FOR FIRST LOVE, HONESTY FOR SINCERITY, WALLFLOWERS FOR FIDELITY THROUGH ADVERSITY, JUDAS TREE FOR BETRAYAL AND SAGE FOR A LONG AND HEALTHY LIFE

The language of flowers

This fragrant bunch of garden blooms makes a lovely, thoughtful gift for an old friend. It also holds an interesting message or two in the language of its flowers which could initiate some very lively reminiscences!

Mixed wallflowers (Erysimum species) purple lilac (Syringa vulgaris), sage flowers (Salvia officinalis), cammassias (Camassia quamash), Honesty flowers (Lunaria annua) and a few branches of flowering judas tree (Cercis siliquastrum).

Spring's warmer days bring the distinct possibility of impromptu meals in the garden. Decorating a table in a sheltered spot has to be equally impulsive. These easy to grow auriculas are a great favourite of mine.

It's so simple to pop a few pots on a table and enjoy them... up close and personal... with a glass of wine and simple food and spend the afternoon watching the wisteria buds begin to open in the warm sun.

Auriculas (Primula auricula), Clematis (Clematis montana 'Elizabeth')

In spite of their exotic appearance, these magnificent
'snake's head fritillaries' are
actually native wild flowers.
Sadly they have become quite
rare in the wild, but they're
widely available in plant
nurseries in late spring.
So here I bought a few pots
and put them in this magnificent copper container to enjoy
indoors before planting in
the garden later. What better
way to help preserve an
endangered species?

Fritillary (Fritillaria meleagris)

SUMMER

And so with the sunshine and the great bursts of leaves growing on the trees, just as things grow in fast movies, I had that familiar conviction that life was beginning over again with the summer.

F. SCOTT FITZGERALD, *The Great Gatsby*

Summer flowers have a glorious voluptuousness that is almost overwhelming. Even their scents are extravagant, and none more so than the incarnation of summertime itself, the rose.

The rose symbolises all the different aspects of love, lust and desire. From the dawn of time it has been linked with goddesses of love and icons of female beauty, from Cleopatra to the Empress Josephine and her famous rose gardens at Malmaison.

Summer's opulence always begins for me with peonies. It's no coincidence that they're often called peony-roses as, with their billowing, frothy petals, they almost overwhelm the real rose.

Geranium and crushed tomato plant leaves both possess delicious scents that take me straight back to childhood. I love mixing them with roses or sweetpeas in arrangements, as I find the combined heady bouquet utterly exhilarating.

Drifts of wildflowers and the lush green tangle of every country lane provide endless inspiration. Add to this the bounty of summer fruits like raspberries, strawberries and jewel coloured currants, and you have the most varied palette any artist could wish for.

I try to capture this soft, overflowing abundance with all my summer flower arrangements and encapsulate the optimism and serenity that permeate the season.

A WILD GARDEN AT DINNER

Ox-eye daisies (Leucanthemum vulgare), poppies (Papaver rhoeas), assorted wild grasses with salad burnet (Sanguisorba minor) and tansy leaves (Tanacetum species) from the herb garden.

I always know summer has arrived when I see
drifts of ox-eye daisies appearing in the
countryside. I like the billowing pillows of
whiteness they create. In fact I like them so
much that I've encouraged them into the wilder
parts of my garden too. A special dinner, either
in the town or in the country, gives the perfect
opportunity to capture the essence of those wild
banks and bring them inside.

The method is one I often use; a collection of
little glass containers holding a few stems placed
asymetrically along a table. This time it's all
linked by a cascade of clematis shoots trimmed
(by necessity) from an over-enthusiastic plant.
Any trailing thing will do. It's like a botanical
silhouette along the dinner table, which is both
unexpected and unconventional.

Roses are the heralds of warm summer days and perhaps the best loved flowers in the world. I'm a fully paid up member of the fan club but infinitely prefer garden roses to anything mass-produced. Admittedly garden varieties have a shorter shelf life and are more difficult to find if you don't have a garden, but they are worth the effort. They have characters as varied as their fanciful names, and here are a few of them... all treated with a distinct approach.

An antique urn of single white roses (rosa 'Rugosa Alba') with white honeysuckle (Lonicera albiflora).

opposite top Three purple glasses contain handfuls of pink roses (rosa 'Constance Spry').

opposite below A coloured glass vase of apricot roses (rosa 'Compassion', 'Warm Wishes' and 'Buff Beauty') and orange honeysuckle (Lonicera tellmanniana).

MIXING FLOWERS WITH UNUSUAL INGREDIENTS, OR PUTTING THEM IN AN UNEXPECTED CONTAINER, CAN CHANGE OUR PERCEPTIONS OF THEM COMPLETELY. A COMBINATION OF GARDEN ROSES AND SUCCULENTS ISN'T PERHAPS A MIXTURE THAT IMMEDIATELY SPRINGS TO MIND. BUT I THINK THERE'S SOMETHING COOL ABOUT THE RESULT, IN EVERY SENSE OF THE WORD.

I IMAGINE THIS TIED WEDDING BOUQUET SUITING A BRIDE WHO WANTS ELEGANT AND CONTEMPORARY FLOWERS. SOMEONE WHO SEES HERSELF AS A MODERN WOMAN, RATHER THAN A ROMANTIC HEROINE AND THEREFORE WANTS HER FLOWERS TO BE NATURAL, UNDERSTATED AND INDIVIDUAL.

(Sedum morganianum 'Burrito') with (rosa 'Margaret Merrill').

A BRIDAL HEADDRESS *following pages*

When Queen Victoria married Prince Albert in 1840, she wore a headdress of orange blossoms to symbolise fruitfulness and fertility. It certainly worked as they produced nine children but it also established a bridal trend that lasted well into the 20th century.

I wanted to capture a vintage 1930s/1940s feel here, and chose Mexican orange blossom and stephanotis. Firstly to imitate real orange blossoms and secondly to produce a similar intoxicating scent.

Mexican orange blossom
(Choisya ternata 'Aztec Pearl')
and stephanotis flowers
(Stephanotis floribunda).

I can
never decide
if *peonies* are
a spring FINALE
or a PRECURSOR
to *summer*

Perhaps it's because they appear in the flower markets long before they open in the cooler climate of the garden. Either way they gently blur the seasonal edges and I quite like that.

Luckily they look wonderful with the last tulips of spring or with the first flowers of summer. Or, and this is my favourite way, completely on their own.

There few flowers so completely sumptuous, and quite frankly, as buxom, as a fully opened double peony . A wide range of beautiful colours gives them very different characters but these exquisite shell pink specimens are without doubt the refined, couture-clad princesses of the peony world.

Five shell pink peonies (Paeonia lactiflora 'Mother's Choice')

PEONIES WITH LILAC *following pages*

Overleaf is a combination in which the flowers, container and setting harmonise together so completely, that the whole piece looks as if it has always been there. This is a confidently subtle look rather than a statement display.

I love lilac for its scent and the romantic softness it adds to the outline of any arrangement and this particular lilac, Maiden's Blush, is one of my favourites. I love the way its pink flush warms the whiteness of these peonies, and loosens the whole outline. The Parian ware jug, in which they both look rather comfortable, sits very naturally on the white marble mantle.

It's very satisfying when this sort of balance is reached in design and I always enjoy the calm comforting sense of serenity it produces.

A jug of lilac (Syringa 'Maiden's Blush') and peonies (Peonia lactifolia 'Festiva Maxima')

Here's a lesson in restraint, and a reminder that less can definitely be much, much more. Each and every stem of these butter-yellow, single peonies is ravishing and so I only needed seven individual specimens, placed into small matching vases, to create this beautiful arrangement. The total picture is so much greater than the sum of its parts, and doesn't, as a result, cost much at all.

Single peony (Paeonia 'Claire de Lune') .

The scent of sweet peas transports me straight back to childhood. Here I've arranged them in a slightly child-like way using some coloured glass tumblers on a sunlit windowsill. In my opinion they just look sad and uncomfortable if they're arranged in a more contrived or sophisticated style. Sweet peas are homely yet delicate country flowers and need no lavish adornment.

Sweetpeas (Lathyrus odoratus hybrids)

When I was a child, our garden in Ireland was full of bright Monkey flowers in summer. We grew both these self-coloured ones and also bright yellow ones with blotches of scarlet 'blood' which I particularly liked.

I saw a tray of plants in a garden nursery and bought some to plant into old cake tins and a wire basket for a brightly coloured retro tea table in the garden. And a trip down memory lane for me!

opposite Growing Monkey Flower plants (Mimulus gutatus)

Summer fruits are far too beautiful to keep hidden in the fridge.

These strawberries look and smell as summer should, and make the simplest sort of decoration for a table. Pretty antique china and a few old teacups with a single rose and stems of strawberry flowers help make the transition from pudding to decoration. Once again, it doesn't require much time or money to achieve this look. Alternatively a black bowl of redcurrants on a scarlet cloth would be as strikingly chic in a contemporary way, and just as economical.

Strawberries, roses (rosa 'Madame Alfred Carriere') and wild strawberry flowers (Fragaria vesca).

I bought this rather bizarre container at auction many years ago.

It's a tulipiere, an odd tiered vase designed to hold stems of tulips.

It looks spectacular on a hall table or a sideboard filled with long stemmed tulips in the spring - as well it should. But I find it works brilliantly with many other flowers too.

Here I've used trails of summer roses in vivid clashing reds, cerise and purple. The tulipiere's shape allows the flowers to trail and tangle in a way a conventional vase wouldn't, and gives height without too much width.

The yellow sitting-room, with its vivid and contrasting colours of turquoise and cherry-red, provides the right backdrop for this arrangement. In fact, it looks thoroughly at home. It certainly shows how an interesting container can have a huge impact on how we appreciate flowers, both as individual specimens and within an overall scheme or setting.

Roses (rosa 'William Baffin', rosa 'William Shakespeare', rosa 'Rugosa') and honeysuckle (Lonicera Periclymenum)

The tulipere on the previous page was a rare and lucky find, but this is something which anyone could copy based on the same principles.

It's simply a modern glass and chrome cake stand with an eclectic collection of glass tumblers and shot glasses on each level. In each 'vase' I placed just a stem or two of small garden flowers. Like the tulipiere, this design has the advantage of creating height easily but by comparison it needs far fewer, shorter flowers to do so.

Sweetpeas (Lathyrus odoratus hybrids) roses (rosa 'Mundi' and rosa 'Pimpinellifolia') chive flowers (Allium schoenoprasum) catmint (Nepeta 'Six Hills Giant') and tellima leaves (Tellima grandiflora 'Forest Frost').

An
eclectic mix
of plants, flowers
and *beautiful* objects
can make a
statement as GRAND
as an
OLD MASTER
painting

This is the sort of thing I really enjoy putting together, and while it's certainly not confined to one season, summer's profusion of plants, flowers and fruit presents many possibilities. There always needs to be a starting point such as a wall colour, fabric or a painting to provide inspiration for the end result.

Then the fun can begin.

In this case the striking wallpaper was my canvas. I knew the ingredients needed to be strong to stand out from such a bold pattern and that exact matches would disappear into it. Instead I chose plants and flowers which I felt had an aesthetic rapport with the colours and shapes behind them. Placed together they merge and yet enhance each other's individual characteristics. Each element acquires more impact as part of the family group. It's certainly a very satisfying way to get some of your favourite things into one single design.

Elephant's ear plant (Alocasia amazonica) Tellima (Tellima grandiflora hybrids) roses (rosa 'Louise Odier') Red valerian (Centhranthus ruber) Lupins (Lupinus 'Inverewe Red') Cardoon leaves (Cynara cardunculus) and fresh cherries.

AUTUMN

On an autumn day in 1987, I embarked upon a full time career in flowers with the illustrious London company of Pulbrook & Gould. Since then the season has held a special nostalgia for me.

I remember bucketfuls of vivid dahlias and glistening bundles of blackberries being delivered on that first day. I also remember the agony of torn fingers as we removed all the blackberry thorns so that customers could arrange them painlessly.

Later in the season came boxes of extraordinary, blistered, ornamental gourds and hard skinned but edible squashes and pumpkins. Branches of crabapples were delivered; their reds, yellows and oranges clashing spectacularly with branches of flaming leaves. The sharp blue of gentians and velvety purple of violets seemed to complement and complete all these vibrant autumnal colours so well.

Autumn...the year's last, loveliest smile

William Cullen Bryant

I also learnt that exuberance is not autumn's only attribute. It can be subdued, with the calm, gentle colours of fading hydrangeas; the milky white and blush pink of snowberries; the parchment shades of mushrooms or the papery browns and buffs of hornbeam and beech.

Autumn is indeed a colourist's dream and I can't resist a painterly approach to all my arrangements: a branch or two of fiery foliage is like an impressionist's doodle in a dull corner. A casual combination of fruit, flowers and foliage becomes an animate still-life for a dinner table.

All this bounty, the product of summer's lengthy days, is nature's dazzling reminder to gather what we can before winter closes in.

THIS MAGICAL TABLE, INSPIRED BY A PRE-RAPHAELITE MASTERPIECE, WOULD MAKE THE PERFECT SETTING FOR ANY SPECIAL CELEBRATION. I'VE INCORPORATED ALL THE SUMPTUOUS COLOURS OF AUTUMN AGAINST THE BACKDROP OF THIS WONDERFULLY ORNATE 1930'S SPEIGEL ('MIRROR') TENT

Visually this table is a sumptuous reminder of the romance and opulence of the Pre-Raphaelite Masters, yet not one of the natural elements I used was expensive or difficult to find.

Ornamental gourds and squashes, hydrangeas, oak leaves and rosehips form the body of the arrangement, with a few bunches of violets in beautiful green glass stemmed bowls to add contrast.

Violets are one of those odd autumn rarities at the flower market. Their deep concentrated colour brings magic to an autumnal mixture. But you don't need many; they are a luxury item and could be replaced with roses or even orchids to give a completely different, more lavish effect.

Dead leaves from the garden, set against the burnished fabric of a sari tablecloth, make the kind of contrast I really enjoy. It also brings in the rural elements of the season which I like to use whenever I can.

With this sort of fantastical scheme, I don't mind a bit of artifice and here I used strands of glass bead blackberries to catch the candlelight and reflect the sari's jewelled embroidery.

The candelabra are bound with sprigs of oak, red rose hips and hydrangea. I use binding wire but you could also try it with garden string as long as you tied a good knot at the end!

All the other elements are just laid casually on the surface of the table. An adventurous gourd can always be held in place with a clump of hydrangea – the latter lasts very well out of water at this time of year.

Hydrangea (Hydrangea macrophylla) ornamental gourds (Cucurbita pepo ovifera various) rosehips (Rosa canina) English oak (Quercus robur) violets (Viola odorata)

This table is as understated as the previous table is sumptuous but the principles guiding my design are exactly the same. Everything is simply placed in a marble bowl with a dribble of water for the rose foliage. The little teal vase of scented jasmine adds the solid contrasting colour, which, for me, is the magical element. I often use mushrooms and fungi in autumn, an idea borrowed from Flemish and Dutch still life paintings. I love the way they give such a sense of the season.

This is a deliciously subtle colour palette, utterly unlike the traditional autumn colours we are so familiar with, which is why I love it. For the arrangement on the previous page, I used beige mushrooms, glaucous green squash, a stem of prickly Scots burnet rose foliage and my favourite washed out hydrangeas. I use them throughout the season and they just seem to pull so many colour schemes together. I can't think how we manage without them for the rest of the year.

Beige oyster mushrooms (Pleurotus ostreatus), hydrangea (Hydrangea macrophylla), rose foliage (rosa 'Pimpinellifolia'), jasmine (Jasminium officinale), ornamental gourds (Cucurbita pepo ovifera various).

Chrysanthemums
receive an
UNJUSTIFIED
bad press,
yet they are the
quintessential autumn flower
&
often locally grown
as well.
So
I use them with
pride.

These bicolour specimens
are
SIMPLY
EXQUISITE

I've put just three of them in one of my favourite containers – an old marble mortar. The stem of ornamental vine from my garden, with its never quite ripe grapes, is a classical painterly touch that gives the whole thing distinction. This would make an effortless and economical arrangement for a supper table.

Chrysanthemum (Chrysanthemum indicum 'Marlen') and grapes (Vitis vinifera ciotat)

Flowers and foliage in autumn can be more elegant and sophisticated than at almost any other time of the year and provide a cornucopia of ideas for a wedding.

It certainly inspired me to create this bridesmaid's headdress. Like a windswept corner of an autumn garden, it's a magical twist of papery oak leaves, fluffy clematis seed heads and scented jasmine. So simple and so natural.

Clematis seed heads (Clematis tanguitica) scented jasmine (Jasminium officinale) and oak leaves (quercus robur)

For the bride, I made this small bouquet of gardenias from the greenhouse and jasmine from the garden. Its scent was intoxicating. I then added one of autumn's prettiest fruits, the white snowberry, to trail from it like strings of pearls. I nearly always recommend a small bridal bouquet rather than a large tied bunch. It complements, rather than competes with the bride's dress, as any well-designed accessory should.

Gardenia (Gardenia thunbergia) scented jasmine (Jasminium officinale) and white snowberry (Symphoricarpos albus 'Constance Spry')

A
flirtation
with *the rules* of scale
proves
an INTERESTING point:
sometimes it's
better not to
try too hard

The chandelier dominating this drawing room is a real design statement as well as piece of contemporary art. Made of hundreds of recycled plastic objects it's an extraordinary size in an ordinary room.

By simply adding five flowers in the same colours, harmony is achieved. Neither fights for attention from the other; the containers even look like they could have fallen out of the chandelier.

I always try to remind myself that innovation isn't simply doing something that's never been done before. That's actually very easy.

Far harder is to build on what exists already and bring another dimension to it, which is what I have aimed to show here.

Two white nerines (Nerine bowdenii alba), one cyclamen flower (Cylamen persicum), one orange dahlia (Dahlia 'Autumn Fairy'), one shocking pink nerine (Nerine 'Zeal Giant').

I JUST CAN'T RESIST THEM.

THIS STUDY IS ABOUT BLENDING BEAUTIFUL CONTAINERS AND INTERESTING CONTENTS AND CONCENTRATING ON TEXTURES AND COLOURS RATHER THAN SHAPE AND LINE. THE MIX OF SMOOTH PURPLE-BLACK WINE GRAPES AND SPIKY GREEN ARTICHOKES REMINDS ME OF ITALY AT THIS TIME OF YEAR. ADD A HANDFUL OF LEAVES, A CARVED URN AND ANTIQUE SERVING DISH, AND YOU HAVE AN EFFORTLESS ITALIANATE STILL LIFE ON THE SUPPER TABLE.

Artichokes (Cynara cardunculus var. scolymus) and grapes (Vitis vinifera)

Autumn is harvest time and everyone who grows vegetables and fruit is overwhelmed (and sometimes exasperated) by nature's bounty.

It's a time to offload excess fruit and vegetables onto non-gardening friends. Think how much more appreciative they'd be if the gifts were presented like this?

I filled this old copper pan with a mosaic of beautiful heritage tomatoes.

But it's the few heads of dahlia and the handful of coppery leaves that add irresistible charm, transforming your surplus into a highly imaginative present.

Heirloom tomato varieties, dahlia (Dahlia 'Unwin Border Red') stephanandra leaves (Stephanandra incisa 'Crispa')

In spite of my many years in the business, I still get great pleasure from giving and receiving flowers and plants as gifts. As we saw with the tomatoes on the previous page, presentation is everything. I'm always looking for old china in car boot sales and junk shops and have a small collection of finds that I can fill with plants or flowers to give to friends.

These old white mixing bowls were a great bargain and make a simple clump of common heather or checkerberry plants look very special.

Caption: White heather (Calluna vulgaris) checkerberry (gaultheria procumbens)

I enjoy using branches of autumn foliage almost as much as branches of blossom in spring. Many are so beautiful and colourful in themselves that I wouldn't dream of adding any flowers. Persian ironwood is a small tree that looks ravishing in its autumn coat. I'd never prune mine at any other time of year.

In this utterly simple arrangement, two cut-off pieces dance across a dressing room table in a clear bottle vase.

Persian ironwood (Parrotia persica)

A FEW STEMS OF CUP AND SAUCER FLOWER

The great flower arranger Constance Spry listed the cup and saucer vine among her favourite flowers, and I can understand why.

The cobea vine is a rampant annual climber that flowers from the end of summer until the first frosts. The unique flowers have great panache and start off a greeny-white colour before fading to this pale puce.

With their unusual shape and certain curiosity value, they're a real conversation piece.

I like to cut a few stems to enjoy indoors and here I mixed them with some tiny pears from an ornamental pear tree and the immature seed heads of garden anemones to make a real botanical study.

Cup and saucer vine (Cobea scandens), ornamental pear (Pyrus salicifolia), garden anemone seed heads(Anemone hupehensis).

GOLDEN AUTUMN LARCH WITH
GOURDS AND HYDRANGEAS *overleaf*

The larch tree in autumn is a joy to behold.

Its needle-like leaves turn the most wonderful shade of buttery gold just before they fall and the season draws to a close.

I love to use both young trees and cut branches in arrangements in those weeks before they lose their flaxen coats.

They look especially good in gilded containers or in gilded rooms so this ornate corner suits them particularly well. I've piled branches into a beautiful old urn with an artistic 'spill' of the most exquisite blue turning green hydrangea heads and some golden yellow gourds.

Hydrangea (Hydrangea 'Double Delights') larch (Larix decidua) gourds (Cucurbita pepo ovifera various)

WINTER

In winter, the smallest bunch of flowers is more welcome than at any other time of year, and plants that show themselves are instantly applauded for their bravery. So I treat them like the rare jewels that they are, often arranging them in delicate stem vases like a Fabergé flower study; or grouping growing plants and bulbs carefully together so that each stem is precious and individual.

I've always been very keen on anything that is willing to flower in cold and wet weather. Perhaps the most extraordinary are scented winter flowering shrubs, for example, wintersweet or winter flowering viburnum, both of which have an enticing fragrance. A small stem of either will fill a room with heart-warming scent.

Hellebores are another passion of mine, both the Christmas and Lenten varieties. I can see why they become so addictive as they defy the harshest conditions to produce flowers of the most magnetic subtlety and charm. Each slight variation in these exquisite flowers can absorb many a gardener's waking hours throughout the winter months. Similarly he or she will enjoy hair-splitting over the seventy-five varieties of that other winter prize, the snowdrop.

Winter continues to provide more surprises with abundant bought flowers such as hyacinths or narcissae. These scented blooms also have a certain delicacy about them and we appreciate and care for them more than we perhaps might at any other time of the year.

Winter is all about arranging with restraint and thoughtfulness; appreciating every single stem and celebrating nature's tenacity and determination.

Winter is the time for comfort, for good food and warmth, for the touch of a friendly hand and for a talk beside the fire: it is the time for home.

Edith Sitwell

A DINNER TABLE WITH BOTANICAL SPECIMENS

Lenten hellebores (Helleborus orientalis hybrids),
Japanese magnolia (Magnolia soulangiana),
witch-hazel (Hammemalis intermedia),
tulips (Tulipa 'black charm'),
snakes head fritillary (Fritillaria meleagris.)
wintersweet (Chimonanthus praecox).

In
the midst of
DARKNESS,
there is always
life.

The table on the previous page is a celebration of that.

Nature doesn't die in winter, it just sleeps, and some things actually flower in those darkest months. I am passionate about winter flowering plants because there's nothing quite like the scent of wintersweet wafting through the air on a frozen morning; or the sight of shell pink petals of a sweet smelling viburnum on a snow covered branch. It's what gets me through the winter.

I like to bring a stem or two inside to appreciate and enjoy. With the right containers and setting, you don't need vast amounts. You can always supplement these rare treasures with a few bought flowers, like the odd mysterious tulip or the first greenhouse grown fritillaries.

left Wintersweet
(Chimonanthus praecox)
right Chinese witch hazel
(Hamamelis mollis)

For me, WINTER is a season of delicate, & often quite subtle beauty

And some of my best-loved flowers begin to appear as the season progresses. The beautiful widow iris, with its subdued charm and delicate perfume is a winter wonder with only a short appearance in the flower market. I like to see a single stem, in a narrow container (seen here) as a living botanical drawing.

Lenten hellebores are amongst my favourite of all, and brave the elements to produce the most exquisite flowers in the garden. A riot of colour they are not, but singly, or in a simple bunch, they have an exotic glamour on a dark day that I find completely irresistible.

Widow iris (Hermodactylus tuberosus) and Lenten hellebores (Helleborus orientalis).

MANY ANCIENT TRADITIONS HAD FESTIVALS
CELEBRATING LIGHT DURING THE DARKEST DAYS
OF WINTER. WHATEVER YOUR SPIRITUAL BELIEFS,
THIS EMPHASIS ON LIGHT CAN ONLY BE A GOOD
THING AND IT'S ALWAYS THE INSPIRATION FOR
MY OWN CHRISTMAS DECORATING.

I particularly like to find things that capture and reflect candlelight and that includes natural ingredients as well as man made ones.

The white berries on the boughs of mistletoe, used here both above and on the surface of the table, glow like pearls in the light. I find that cut glass reflects light in the most dramatic way, and I capitalize on this by using engraved storm lanterns and hanging antique chandelier drops on the branches above.

Boughs of mistletoe (Viscum album) lichen covered branches, pine (Pinus varieties) pots of jasmine (Jasminium polyanthum) and candle light.

Christmas is the time of year when everyone's design philosophies suddenly materialise. We're bombarded with decoration ideas, gift-wrapping ideas and tree ornament designs from the end of summer. By December, the result is often a muddle of unrelated schemes. Which is completely fine if that's what you want (I loathe the designer snobbishness that appears at Christmas and sets rules about what is tasteful or not) but sometimes it's good to step back and work out what you really DO want.

Personally I want light and simplicity. I like to draw on the Northern European tradition of bringing evergreens indoors, but I also like the idea of light and sparkle too, so I can embrace glass and glitter with the best of them. But my starting point is always nature, whether it is the delicacy of a skeletonised leaf touched with gold, or a lichen covered branch to hang sparkling ornaments from.

MANY
YEARS AGO,
I made a wedding bouquet
of *snowdrops*
&
*I've
never
forgotten
it.*

I have tried to recreate that memory here. And it was a rewarding labour of love: tiny bunches of snowdrops were individually wired into clumps of fresh moss, then assembled into this tremblingly beautiful bouquet with a delicate silk covered handle.

A tied bunch of snowdrops would be entirely different; the flowers would, by necessity, be more tightly bound, and lose any freedom to echo the movements of the bride.

I love the sheer jewel-like exquisiteness of it, and the fact it's so seasonal one couldn't ever guarantee it for any particular wedding date, makes it even more desirable. Snowdrops symbolise consolation and hope in the language of flowers and I think any winter bride would be very lucky to have them.

Double snowdrops (Galanthus nivalis 'flore pleno')

This beautiful china 'flower brick' is, in a way, the younger cousin of the tulipiere on page 78. Both were hugely popular vases in the 18th Century and I can see why: it's incredibly easy to arrange flowers in them. Just add water and put flower stems through the evenly spaced holes on top. As simple as doing a dot-to-dot picture.

They are especially good for 18th Century inspired mixed collections of flowers like this one.

Wintersweet (Chimonanthus praecox), witch hazel (Hamamelis mollis), stinking iris seed pods (Iris foetidissima), hyacinth (Hyacinthus 'Jan Bos'), Viburnum bodnantense and Garrya elliptica.

Bundles of varicoloured dogwood stems are a mainstay of winter flower markets, but try them as a growing plant too. This beautiful variety has been described as a 'twig bonfire' and was a Christmas present to me from a great friend. It joined us for the celebrations inside (along with these bemused Chinese deer) and now it's happily growing in the garden...

Dogwood plant (Cornus sanguinea 'Midwinter Fire')

ONE OF THE JOYS OF GROWING
BULBS INDOORS IN WINTER IS
THAT THEY ENCAPSULATE AND
ANTICIPATE THE NEWNESS OF
SPRING AND IT'S SENSE OF
REVITALIZATION. ITS THE MIRACLE
THAT EVERY GARDENER RECOGNISES
HAVING PLANTED IN BLIND FAITH
IN THE AUTUMN. GROWING BULBS
AND EARLY SPRING PLANTS INDOORS
STARTS THE PLEASURE EVEN EARLIER
WHILE THE GARDEN OUTSIDE IS
STILL LOCKED IN WINTER

These days we can be lazy, and buy planted bulbs which are about to flower, particularly hyacinths and narcissae. For their mesmerizing scent alone I happily support this, but you do miss out on those early weeks of anticipation. I sometimes wash the soil off flowering bulbs and make the whole root system part of the decoration-seen through a clear glass of water or spilling over moss in a pot. A bowl of flowering bulbs or seasonal plants like these Christmas roses make perfect Christmas presents.

Using a lilac tree, forced to flower in a greenhouse in winter, does appear to contradict all my seasonal proselytizing.

Apparently the last Empress of Russia, Alexandra, was so fond of lilac that it was grown for her in the vast imperial greenhouses throughout the year. Perhaps she needed some of nature's simple beauty to nurture her soul through the interminable coldness of a Russian winter, and possibly I empathise with her in my willingness to bend my own rules on this occasion.

For all of us winter should be the season for treats and a little decadence. The scent and stark, sculptural beauty of the lilac can be enjoyed during the dark days and then planted outside in spring.

A forced white lilac tree (Syringa vulgaris)

This marble bowl of growing snowdrops is an intimate and restrained botanical study. It looks like it might have been dug up from the forest floor, a growing painting of earth and flowers.

In reality it was all put together with a few pots of snowdrops and some natural 'props' like moss, dead rose sprigs and some wild ivy. These painterly compositions make us all look more closely at our favourite flowers and their natural habitats and patterns of growth. Only then can we really begin to learn how to make flowers and plants look natural and beautiful in our home.

Snowdrops (Galanthus nivalis)

Cyclamen are incredibly popular winter houseplants. They deserve to be as they are so easy to grow and have a broad colour range. Large trays of flowery cyclamen plants seem irresistible, but a few lonely pots seldom look as good when you get them home. Then I discovered a new way of enjoying them: I harvest the flowers and use them for cut arrangements instead. They last very well; the plant keeps producing flowers on a windowsill out of sight; and I can have little vases to enjoy around the house. Somehow these small but intense clusters of flowers capture the enticing vibrancy of the potted versions en masse.

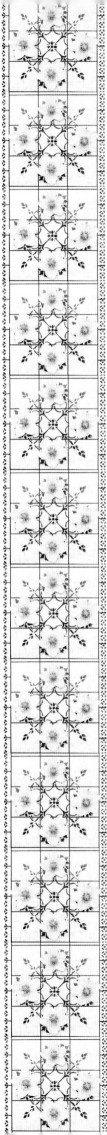

In
many ways,
this simple little
vase of
SNOWDROPS
and
CHRISTMAS
ROSES
summarises
my theories of
flower arranging:

Simply choose a few compatible flowers (in this case two great favourites, snowdrops and Christmas roses), fill a container with water and then let the flowers arrange themselves.

It really is that simple.

The choice of which flowers and which container is a very individual thing, but there are no rules. I was inspired here by the worn flaky paintwork, which seemed to suit these ancient garden flowers. The lustre vase in turn seemed to echo the fluted pilasters and hint at winter frosts in the garden.

It's all about harmony, and this is certainly playing my favourite tune.

Christmas roses (Helleborus niger), double snowdrops (Galanthus nivalis 'flore pleno')

FACT: you can never have too many containers.

The containers you choose for plants or flowers are almost as important as the plants or flowers themselves. A container can emphasise peculiar natural qualities by holding the stem in a particular way; or intensify a flower's subtle hues with its own lustre.

Containers also link the flowers to their environment and help them look like part of a particular décor.

They can also help create a mood or theme for special events.

On a superficial level, containers make the whole process fun and creative because, with the right one, flowers really can arrange themselves. Buy ones that suit you; and buy ones that catch your attention, for whatever reason – quirky, country, classy or kitsch.

On the opposite page you'll see some of my collection, and I'd like to mention a few shapes that I do find especially useful:

SMALL BOTTLES that hold single stems, in clear or coloured glass, work well with tiny delicate things. Taller decanters will hold a larger stem or branch. They make flowers look like botanical specimens.

WIDER TOPPED VASES in glass or copper. These are perfect for bunches of bought flowers or garden collections alike. They hold lots of water, essential for larger bunches which need it.

NARROW NECKED JUGS hold things together in a way the wider ones don't. Garden flowers especially seem to have a natural affinity with jugs.

COLOURED GLASS can completely increase the intensity of flowers and foliage alike. Turquoise glass in particular, flatters any flower.

BOWLS LARGE AND SMALL are great for floating or heaping together broken off flower heads. Fruit too.

QUIRKY CONTAINERS like the Buddah foot and the pewter inkwell are just a bit of fun. They do hold flowers wonderfully but also remind us not to take it all too seriously.

Nowadays we all agree that, when it comes to food, we should be sourcing the best quality ingredients from local producers. It's exactly the same with plants and flowers, and a little bit of common sense goes a long way to helping them last and give of their best in your house.

CUT FLOWERS FROM THE GARDEN

Use sharp scissors or secateurs to make a clean cut. A torn stem won't absorb water as easily.

In the interests of both appearance and preservation of the plant, cutting at the bottom of a stem or back to a leaf joint is good practice. The plant recovers more quickly and you won't have left an ugly stump.

Try to cut in a cooler part of the day, or when the sun is not shining directly on the flowers.

If possible place immediately into a bucket of water. If not, put the stems in a shady place as you gather more.

Never cut multi-petalled flowers like roses when they are fully opened or when they're wet from rain. They simply won't last.

BUYING CUT FLOWERS OR PLANTS

Always try to to buy locally grown and sourced produce.

Make sure you select the best quality plants and flowers that have been well looked after.

With plants look for strong growth, disease-free leaves and damp soil in the pot.

With flowers, look particularly for firm blooms (preferably not fully open) unblemished petals and healthy leaves.

Try to buy at the end of a shopping trip so that the flowers or plants don't have to wait in a hot car for too long.

WHEN YOU GET THEM INSIDE

Someone once said that cut flowers and houseplants should be treated like guests: when they arrive, offer them a strong drink and a bath and let them have a good rest before expecting them to do anything. So when you bring them in from the garden or take them out of the car try the following:

Remove any leaves that might sit below water otherwise they'll rot and make the water smell horrible. Then cut the stem at an angle with sharp scissors and place in a bucket of deep, cold water. Allow to rest in a cool room for a few hours to acclimatise and recover.

Flowers with very woody stems such as lilacs may benefit from having the bottom few centimetres crushed to expose more fibres to the water. Bashing them carefully with a hammer on a hard surface will do the trick.

Flowering shrubs, with a disproportionate amount of leaf to flower, will last longer if they have a high percentage of their leaves removed. Again lilacs, or mock orange blossom, are good examples.

Hellebores and euphorbias behave better if they're placed in a bucket with about 3cm of freshly boiled water. When it cools, simply add cold water to the usual height.

Cutting the stems and putting them into warm water can also revive wilting flowers.

With houseplants, check the care instructions or look them up online. Find out where they will be happiest in terms of light and heat and how much water they need. It's that easy. There are no generalizations with growing plants although few will thrive in constant intense heat or darkness.

ARRANGING THE FLOWERS AND PLANTS

Now that they have been given a chance to rest and acclimatise (I would suggest overnight or for a few hours at least) you can take the plants and flowers and be creative.

The section on vases and containers will help you choose a suitable thing to put them in but for cut flower arrangements, always pick something that holds enough water for the amount of stems you are putting in it. Cut flowers and foliages drink more water in the first 24 hours so always remember to top up water levels.

Always re-cut each stem immediately before placing it in the vase of water, and always look at care instructions for growing plants used inside before choosing where to put them.

Never place any arrangements near direct sources of heat or light.

ACKNOWLEDGMENTS

This book was very much a team effort and Jason Lowe, Lawrence Morton, Jo Woodhouse and Mark Lovegrove deserve equal credit for the result.

As does Catharine Snow who so patiently edited, guided (and fed) the team throughout and commissioned it in the first place.

We'd all like to thank the following people for kindly allowing us to photograph in their houses and gardens:

Lassco, Vauxhall Bridge Road, David Ross and Emma Pilkington, Jolyon and Kirsty Luke, Hugh and Samantha Godsal, Baron Augustin von Hochschild, Count and Countess Manfredi della Gherardesca, Eric and Cassandra Wetter and Andrea Hamilton.

I would like to thank my business partner Jamie Marlar, his wife Patricia and the wonderful 'Shane Connolly troupe' for keeping the show on the road: Mark Lovegrove, Tracey Gorton, Moira Seedhouse, Julie Mac Phillips, Michele Baroni, Brigitte Girling, Louise Avery, Graham Murtough, Clare McKnight, Anita Everard and Paul Williams and the team at Pollencrew (with constant backstage support from Stephen Smallwood and all at Thorne Widgery)

A special thanks to my flower suppliers: David Gorton (GB Foliage) Dennis Edwards (Alagar) Pratley and co, Bloomfield and Co, Quality Plants, Arnott and Mason, C.Best, L.Mills, Evergreen, Frank Matthews (Trees for Life) and Danae Brook (Country Roses)

I would like to express my gratitude to the following people for their inspiring and pivotal support: Michael Goulding and Elizabeth Barker, Pulbrook and Gould, Caroline Evans, Margaret and Mervyn Boyd, Regina Rickless, Sylvia Took, TRH the Prince of Wales and the Duchess of Cornwall and HRH the Duchess of Cambridge.

And finally...huge thanks to my family for their constant love and encouragement and most especially my darling wife Candida who makes everything worthwhile.